world breads

world breads

FROM PAIN DE CAMPAGNE TO PARATHA

PAUL GAYLER

with photography by RICHARD JUNG

CASTLE BOOKS

This edition published in 2011 by
CASTLE BOOKS (R)
a division of BOOK SALES, INC.
276 Fifth Avenue Suite 206
New York, New York 10001
USA

This edition published by arrangement with Jacqui Small, an imprint of Aurum
Press Limited, 7 Greenland St, London, NW1 0ND

First published in 2006 by Jacqui Small.

Publisher   Jacqui Small
Editor   Madeline Weston
Art Director   Ashley Western
Food stylist   Linda Tubby
Props stylist   Roisin Nield
Production   Peter Colley

ISBN-13: 978-0-7858-2768-9

10 9 8 7 6 5 4 3 2 1

Printed and bound in China

Half title Broa, see page 16
Title page Pan-Asian Cob, see page 41
Imprint page Grissini, see page 50
Contents page Turkish stuffed pillow bread, see page 53
Endpapers Classic Baguette, see page 26

contents

basic ingredients

WHEAT FLOURS

Bread is basically a mixture of flour, water, and yeast, and it is the flour that accounts for the differences in the flavor in the wide variety of breads available. Flours vary in taste, strength, and texture, the strength depending on the amount of gluten (protein) they contain.

WHITE FLOUR

Has a high gluten content, it is ground from wheat grains with outer bran and wheat germ removed. It absorbs water readily and produces a good elastic-like dough when kneaded.

WHITE BREAD FLOUR

This comes from hard wheat with a high proportion of gluten. Gluten allows a dough to expand, gives added structure and strength, and enables it to rise.

ALL-PURPOSE AND SELF RISING FLOURS

These are not often used in bread making as the lack of gluten does not produce a good loaf.

WHOLE-WHEAT FLOUR

Also known as wholemeal or whole-grain flour, it is made from the entire wheat grain including wheat germ and bran. It contains gluten, so can be used instead of white flour. However breads made using only whole-wheat flour tend to be coarser and heavier than white bread, so most whole wheatbreads are made with a proportion of white bread flour.

OTHER FLOURS – RYE FLOUR

Next to white and whole-wheat, rye is the most popular flour for bread making. It is dark, dense, and comes in various forms such as light rye, medium rye, and dark rye. Dark rye is often mixed with white flour to give a lighter loaf.

GRANARY FLOUR

This flour is a blend of brown flour and rye flour and is available in supermarkets and health stores.

MALTHOUSE FLOUR

A blend of stone-ground brown flour, rye, and malted wheat flour. Similar to granary flour.

MISCELLANEOUS FLOURS AND MEALS

Products milled from other grains are occasionally used to add variety, used in combination with white flour. They include cornmeal, rice flour, buckwheat flour, soy flour, oat flour, and barley flour. Meal is not as finely ground as flour.

LEAVENING AGENTS

All leavening agents cause the incorporation of gases in a loaf to increase volume, and produce shape and texture. Exact measurements of leavening agents are important. Yeast, baking powder, and baking are all forms of leavening agents.

YEAST

Yeast is a single-celled organism which when given warmth and food (flour, sugar, potato etc), ferments and gives off carbon dioxide as it does so. Overheating yeast can kill it and spoil the dough.

Fresh yeast will keep for up to 7 days well wrapped in the refrigerator, several months if kept frozen. I suggest buying it from small bakers or health stores, although some super-markets do stock it. Fresh yeast should be fresh looking, break into pieces with a snap and should smell fresh. It is crumbled into a small bowl along with a pinch of sugar. Pour over a little warm water or milk to form a smooth paste then add to the dry ingredients.

Active dry yeast is also used in bread making, it is best stored in an airtight container and ideally used within 2–3 months. Stale yeast smells musty and will not produce a frothy appearance when mixed with a liquid; it is best thrown away. To use dry yeast, sprinkle the granules into a bowl with a pinch of sugar. Pour on the warm liquid and stir well. Allow it to absorb the water and leave for 10–15 minutes until it becomes frothy.

'Rapid rise yeast' can be added directly to the flour at the beginning, then the warm liquid is poured on to form a dough. As a general rule these breads require only one rising.

It is not possible to simply substitute the different yeasts fresh for dried as they all act differently, but below are the equivalents:-

For a 1lb flour mix use either:-

$3/4$ oz fresh yeast, $1^{1}/2$ tsp active dry or 1 x 7g envelope rapid rise yeast.

SALT
Salt strengthens gluten structure, making the dough more elastic, thus improving the bread's texture. It also inhibits yeast growth, controlling fermentation in the dough and preventing the growth of undesirable wild yeasts. Generally 1–2 teaspoons per 1lb flour is about right; never add salt directly to the water in which yeast is softened.

LIQUIDS
Water is the best liquid for plain bread doughs, giving a better, crustier finish, although milk can also be used. Milk adds texture, crust, color and nutritional value as well as flavor in enriched breads.

The liquid should be hand hot (about 90F°) to encourage yeast growth and fermentation. When fermentation takes place at too high a temperature unpleasant flavors are produced. Too hot and the liquid will kill the yeast – too cold and the bread will take longer to proof. A good guide for the correct heat is to mix one third boiling water with two thirds cold water.

In some countries beer is sometimes used as the liquid, giving the bread a maltier taste.

Because gluten must absorb liquid before it can be developed, the amount used can affect the texture of the bread. All flours vary in the amount they absorb, for example, whole-wheat flour and rye flour will absorb liquid more readily than white flour.

FATS
The major functions of fat used in bread making are firstly to add flavor, moisture and richness and secondly to increase keeping qualities. Either butter or lard and occasionally olive oil are used.

Fat slows down yeast action, therefore the rising will be less then in plain doughs.

EGGS
Eggs and protein add structure to baked goods as well as richness, flavor and color to doughs. Eggs also have the added benefit in improving shelf life in enriched breads.

SWEETENERS
Most recipes require a small amount of sweetener to feed the yeast, add flavor to the dough, help crust color and increase keeping qualities. White sugar is the most frequently used but honey, malt extract, and molasses can also be used.

Sugar is often added to fresh yeast at the beginning. When using active dry yeast, it is best to follow the recipe for its inclusion. Sugar slows down the action of yeast and most sweet recipe doughs call for more yeast and a longer proving time.

FLAVORINGS AND TOPPINGS
All manner of flavorings may be added to both sweet and regular breads, incorporated into the dough during the kneading process. Topping bread with a different interesting nuts and seeds adds variety, and texture to bread as well as supplementary vitamins and minerals.

basic step by steps

1 Sift the flour and salt in a large mixing bowl, make a well in the center and add the yeast liquid at once. Bring it together using one hand to form a light soft sticky dough. Add more flour if necessary, and work the dough until it is smooth and leaving the sides of the bowl. Turn out onto a lightly floured surface.

2 Gather the dough into a ball with the tips of your fingers, then fold it towards you. While pressing down on it, push it away from you with the palm of your hand, stretching it as you do so. Give the dough a quarter turn and repeat until it feels firm and elastic (about 10 minutes).

3 Place the dough in a lightly oiled bowl, cover it with plastic wrap or a damp cloth, and leave in a warm place until it has doubled in size.

4 and 5 Turn the dough onto the work surface.

6 Knock out the air bubbles to ensure a good well risen bread and even texture. This is called 'knocking back' or 'punching down' the dough.

7 Shape the dough into the desired shape, place on a baking sheet, dust it with flour, and set aside for the second rising (proving).

8 Make slashes or cuts on the top of the dough to help the bread expand during cooking and give an attractive finish.

9 To test if the bread is cooked, turn it out and tap it gently on the base. It should sound hollow.

10 Transfer the bread to a cooling rack; this allows the escape of excess moisture and stops the bread from becoming soggy.

types of dough making processes

BASIC STRAIGHT DOUGH (SHORT FERMENTATION)

Most home-baked breads are made by the simple 'straight dough' method, where the flour, yeast, and water are mixed together at the beginning. Although this produces a very acceptable loaf, it does not compare with breads made using a starter dough.

STARTER DOUGHS (PRE-FERMENTATION)

Many European-style breads are made using a starter dough. Dough composed of flour, water, and a small quantity of yeast is left to ferment then added to the other ingredients. Pre-ferments enable the yeast to start working in advance and give a light acidity. Different pre-ferments vary by the amount of water the dough contains. In the SPONGE method, yeast is dissolved in more warm water than usual, then mixed with some of the flour from the recipe to make a sloppy batter. This is left at least 30 minutes or until bubbles appear which aerate the dough.

Named after Polish bakers, POOLISH is similar to sponging but uses equal amounts of flour and water making a thicker batter. It is left from 2–12 hours, giving a wonderful light acidity to the bread, a milder flavor and a good crisp crust.

BIGA is the Italian term for pre-ferment, and its consistency is more akin to a classic bread dough, and is the strongest in terms of gluten. It is usually made 12 to 24 hours in advance and generally used within 3 days. (It may be frozen up to 3 months).

A NOTE ON SOURDOUGH

Before commercial yeasts, bread was often started by a simple mixing of flour and water left to stand until wild yeasts settled on it and began to ferment it. However, now sourdough is generally started with the addition of a little commercial yeast. The starter can be kept in the refrigerator for up to 10 days (longer if frozen), where it will become progressively more acidic.

KNEADING

Kneading the dough is undoubtedly the most important step of the whole process – it strengthens and develops the dough, enabling it to rise. It can be done in a food processor or mixer, as well as by hand.

When using a food processor, the basic dough is made in the processor fitted with a dough blade until the dough comes together. Kneading on full speed generally takes 1 minute, followed by 2–3 minutes by hand.

1   2   3   4   5

If using an electric mixer, make the dough as usual and transfer it to the mixer fitted with a dough hook, and knead it on full speed for 2–3 minutes.

A well made and properly kneaded dough should look plump, well rounded and have a smooth almost satiny surface.

RISING
The dough should be allowed to rise slowly for 1–2 hours in a draft free area at a temperature between 70–80°F. It can also be left to rise slowly in the refrigerator overnight – this allows the enzymes and starches more time to mature. This is typical of some of the world's greatest breads, the French baguette for example.

KNOCKING BACK, DIVIDING, AND SECOND RISING
Following the dough's rising, turn it out onto a work surface. If making 2 loaves, cut the dough in half with a sharp knife. Cover one half with a damp cloth or plastic wrap to keep it moist while you work the other.

After 'knocking back' or 'punching down' the dough is divided into rolls or shaped as desired, placed on baking sheets, or in special molds ready for the second rising known as 'proving'; this tests the yeast is alive and active. Proving also ensures there will be an even rise during baking.

SHAPING AND FORMING THE BREAD
For me, shaping the dough is perhaps the most rewarding part of the whole bread making experience, but for many it can be a worry. Breads when not mold baked should look a little rough and free form. When handling and shaping dough you need to be firm yet gentle, so as not to tear the gluten.

BAKING IN MOLDS AND PANS
Breads baked in a loaf pan or mold have the pan to maintain their shape. Batter doughs can be cooked in cake pans, earthenware dishes, even deep skillets.

Loaf pans should be about twice the size of the prepared dough and a new loaf pan should be well greased. After the initial baking, it is best simply wiped clean. I use non-stick black baking pans as they absorb the heat better, giving a crisper finish.

To fill a bread pan, roll out the dough to a rectangle, a little longer than the pan, then fold it in half lengthwise, pinching the edges together on the sides. Flatten the dough slightly your hand, fold the dough over once more and pinch the edges together again.

Roll the dough backwards and forwards to form a well rounded shape, tuck in both ends, then place in the pan with the seam running along the bottom. Cover the loaf and set aside to proof.

GLAZING AND FINISHING
Glazing gives an attractive finish and introduces moisture during baking. Bread can also be glazed after baking. Glazes include eggs, egg white, milk, butter, olive oils, and sweet sugar syrups in the case of sweetened breads.

For a crisp crust and unglazed look, brush or spray with cold water or lightly dust with flour before baking. For a matt crust and unglazed look, brush with sunflower or light olive oil.

Brush with beaten egg wash or a mixture of egg yolk and cream or milk for a richer flavor. For a slightly salty crust, brush with a mixture of egg white whisked lightly with a pinch or two of salt. This also gives the bread a slightly thicker crust.

BAKING
Whether you bake your bread in a gas or electric oven it must be thoroughly preheated. Professional bakers have steam injected ovens which improve the texture in hard crusted breads. In home baking, place a dish in the base of the oven, then add some ice cubes to create steam.

Enriched doughs do not form crisp crusts and are usually baked without steam. Always cook bread thoroughly, it is better to overcook than to undercook it.

6   7   8   9   10

classic breads

ciabatta

ITALIAN SLIPPER BREAD

This popular deli bread can be made into small loaves to fill with all manner of wonderful ingredients. The dough itself is fairly wet but makes a chewy crust after baking.

INGREDIENTS
MAKES 3 LOAVES

FOR THE *BIGA* STARTER
3 cups white bread flour, plus a little for dusting
1 1/2 tsp active dry (1/3 oz fresh) yeast
scant 1 cup warm water

FOR THE DOUGH
1 1/2 tsp active dry (1/2 oz fresh) yeast
1 3/4 cup warm water
4 1/2 cups white bread flour
1 tsp fine sea salt
2 tbsp olive oil

1   Sift the flour for the starter into a large bowl. In a small bowl dissolve the yeast in scant 1/2 cup of the warm water, leave for 10 minutes until frothy.

2   Gradually mix the dissolved yeast and the remaining water into the flour to form a soft but firmish dough. Turn out the dough onto a lightly floured surface, knead for 5 minutes until pliable.

3   Return to the bowl, cover with plastic wrap and leave in a warm place to proof for 10–12 hours, by which time the dough will have begun to collapse.

4   For the dough, mix the yeast with scant 1/2 cup of the warm water, leave to stand for 5 minutes then add the remaining water.

5   Add the yeast mixture into the *biga* starter and beat it in with one hand. Beat in the flour with your hand to form a wet mix. Finally beat in the salt and olive oil. Cover with plastic wrap, leave in a warm place for 1 hour 30 minutes.

6   Spoon the dough onto a prepared large baking sheet, liberally dusted with flour. Using floured hands, shape into oval shaped loaves, about 1 inch thick. Leave to proof again for a further 25 minutes.

7   Preheat the oven to 425°F. Place in the oven on a center shelf to bake for 25–30 minutes, until golden and cooked. Transfer to a cooling rack.

white soda bread

Traditionally Irish soda bread was baked on a hot griddle over an open fire to obtain a wonderful crisp crust. It is best eaten straight from the oven, or at least on the day it is made.

INGREDIENTS
MAKES 1 LOAF

4 1/2 cups all-purpose flour
1 tsp baking soda
1 tsp fine sea salt
1 1/2–1 2/3 cups buttermilk or
half milk/half plain yogurt

1   Preheat the oven to 425°F. Sieve the dry ingredients into a large bowl and make a well in the center. Pour most of the buttermilk in at once to mix to a soft dough using one hand. Add more buttermilk if necessary: the dough should be softish, but not wet and sticky in texture.

2   Turn out onto a lightly floured surface, knead lightly for 30 seconds – the more gently the dough is handled, the lighter the bread will be.

3   Shape the dough into a round, about 1 inch thick, and place on a lightly floured baking sheet. Cut a cross, 3/4 inch deep, on the top of the loaf, ensuring the cuts go over the sides of the dough too.

4   Place in the oven and bake for 20 minutes, then reduce heat to 375°F and cook for a further 15 minutes or until cooked and golden. Transfer to a cooling rack to cool slightly before eating.

date and pecan bread

Dates were popular in Britain in Elizabethan times when dried fruits and nuts were imported to satisfy the market for new and exotic produce. This loaf originally used walnuts, but I find pecans a better balance for the sweet dates. This is great for serving with cheese.

1   Place the flour and salt in a large mixing bowl, add the yeast and make a well in the center. Pour in the warm water and milk and bring together with one hand to form a soft dough. Turn out onto a lightly floured surface and knead for 8–10 minutes until smooth and elastic.

2   Place in a lightly oiled bowl, cover with plastic wrap, leave to proof in a warm place for 1 to 1^{1}/$_{2}$ hours or until doubled in size.

3   Turn out onto a floured surface again. Knock back to expel the air. Add the flour dusted dates and the pecans and knead for 2 minutes, then roll into a plump round loaf. Place on a baking sheet, on in a loaf pan, cover with a cloth, and leave to rise again in a warm place for 40 minutes.

4   Preheat the oven to 400°F. Spray or brush the loaf with water then dust liberally with granary or malthouse flour. Bake on a center shelf for 15 minutes, then reduce the heat to 375°F and bake for a further 20 minutes until cooked and golden. Transfer to a cooling rack.

INGREDIENTS
MAKES 1 LOAF

3^{1}/$_{2}$ cups granary or malthouse flour
2 tsp fine sea salt
1^{1}/$_{2}$ tsp active dry yeast
^{1}/$_{2}$ cup plus 1 tbsp warm water
^{1}/$_{2}$ cup plus 1 tbsp warm milk
1 cup fresh dates, stoned, chopped
    and mixed with 1 tbsp flour
1 cup chopped pecans

CARAMEL AND BROWN BREAD ICE CREAM

Place 6 egg yolks and ^{1}/$_{4}$ cup of sugar in a bowl, whisk until pale and creamy. Place 2^{3}/$_{4}$ cups light cream and 1 split vanilla pod into a pan, warm over a low heat.

For the caramel, place scant ^{1}/$_{2}$ cup of sugar along with 2 tbsp water and a pinch of salt in a pan. Cook over a medium heat, stirring until the sugar dissolves. Without stirring, increase the heat to high and boil until the syrup turns to a dark amber-colored caramel.

Remove from the heat and, taking care, pour in the cream. Pour half this hot caramel mixture onto the egg mixture. Return the egg mixture to the pan containing the remaining caramel and cook it until it begins to thicken but do not let it boil. Strain, and allow to cool.

Toast 6 oz date and pecan bread, cut into small cubes, under a hot broiler until golden. Mix the bread cubes with the ice cream base and churn the mixture. Freeze in an ice cream/sorbet maker following the manufacturer's instructions.

seeded granary baton

A wonderfully healthy bread which you can vary with the vast range of grains and seeds available in health food stores. It can also be baked in a pan, lightly greased with vegetable oil.

INGREDIENTS
MAKES 2 LOAVES

2½ cups whole-wheat flour or granary flour
1¾ cups white bread flour
2 tsp fine sea salt
1½ tsp active dry (⅓ oz fresh) yeast
2 tsp clear honey
1¼ cups warm water
1 tbsp sunflower seeds
1 tbsp pumpkin seeds
2 tsp sesame seeds

1 Mix both flours with the salt in a large mixing bowl.

2 In a small bowl, mix the yeast with the honey and half the warm water until smooth. Add the remaining water and mix to form a soft dough. Turn out the dough onto a lightly floured surface and knead for 8–10 minutes until smooth and elastic. Add the sunflower and pumpkin seeds to the dough and knead for a further minute.

3 Place the dough in a lightly oiled bowl, cover with plastic wrap and leave to proof for 1 to 1½ hours.

4 Turn out the dough again and knock back to expel the air. Divide the dough into two. Shape the dough into two batons. Spray or brush with water then roll the tops in sesame seeds until well coated, pressing in the seeds gently. Place on a lightly floured baking sheet, cover, and leave in a warm place for a further 30 minutes.

5 Preheat the oven to 375°F. Bake on the center shelf for 30–35 minutes until golden and crisp. Transfer to a cooling wire to cool.

broa

PORTUGUESE COUNTRY BREAD

This recipe is my version of the bread enjoyed all over Portugal and that I have often bought there. Called *broa* — made of cornmeal with a crisp olive oil crust — it is simple to prepare.

INGREDIENTS
MAKES 2 LOAVES

1½ tsp active dry (¾ oz fresh) yeast
1¾ cups warm water
2½ cups cornmeal, plus a little for dusting
3¾ cups white bread flour
2 tbsp good quality olive oil, plus a little for brushing
1 tsp fine sea salt

1 Place the yeast in a bowl, pour over 1 cup plus 2 tbsp of the water, then mix until blended. Add half the cornmeal and ½ cup of the flour to make a sponge starter, with batter consistency.

2 Cover the bowl with plastic wrap, and leave to stand for 45 minutes or until bubbles form and it becomes light and fluffy in appearance. Stir in the remaining water and the olive oil.

3 Add the remaining cornmeal and flour, the salt, then bring together to form a soft dough. Turn out the dough onto a lightly floured table, knead for 10 minutes until smooth and pliable. Place in a lightly oiled bowl, cover with plastic wrap, and leave to rise in a warm place for up to 1 hour or until doubled in size.

4 Turn out the dough again and knock back to expel the air. Shape into two round loaves and lightly flatten with one hand. Place on a lightly floured baking sheet, cover, and return to a warm place to rise for another hour until doubled in size again.

5 Preheat the oven to 450°F. Brush the loaves with olive oil and lightly dust with cornmeal then slash in a chequerboard pattern (see page 1). Bake for 15 minutes then reduce the heat to 425°F and cook for a further 20 minutes until golden and cooked. Transfer to a cooling rack.

Broa is illustrated on page 1.

german beer bread

BEER BROT

The Germans are particularly proud of their beers and rightly so! Used in bread making, beer has natural yeasty flavor that contributes to great bread. Here is a typical beer bread, which I first tasted some years ago, made by one of my German chefs — delicious served with all manner of cheeses.

1 Place the rye flour in a large mixing bowl with the yeast.

2 Heat the beer along with the water to 85°F. Make a well in the center of the flour. Pour in the warmed liquid and bring the mix to a batter-like dough with one hand. Add the caraway seeds.

3 Cover the bowl with plastic wrap, and leave to proof at room temperature for 1 to 1½ hours.

4 Gradually incorporate the white flour and salt then turn out and knead well for 5–6 minutes until soft and pliable. Place in a clean, lightly oiled bowl, cover again, and leave in a warm place to proof and double in size.

5 Preheat the oven to 375°F. Turn out the dough and knock back to expel the air. Shape into three well greased 2lb loaf pans, then brush or spray with water and dust liberally with rye flour. Using a sharp knife make 5 slashes across the top of the loaves about 5mm ¼ inch deep.

6 Place in the oven on the center shelf for 10–15 minutes. Reduce the heat to 350°F and bake for a further 20 minutes until cooked. Transfer to a cooling rack.

VARIATIONS

For that added light crunchy texture and mellow flavor, replace the caraway seeds with 2 tbsp of sunflower seeds.

INGREDIENTS
MAKES 3 LOAVES

1¾ cups light rye flour,
  plus a little for dusting
1½ tsp active dry yeast
275ml light German beer (e.g. Becks)
¾ cup warm water
1 tbsp caraway seeds
4½ cups white bread flour
2 tsp fine sea salt

OPEN SANDWICH TOPPINGS

Sliced beer bread makes a great base for German-style open sandwiches — topped with all manner of wonderful ingredients. Top the bread with some of the following:

Smoked salmon, horseradish cream, and dill

Folded Black Forest ham with mustard, mayonnaise, and asparagus tips

Matjes-style herrings with sliced apple, red onion, and mayonnaise

Various sliced cured meats with herb mustard, sliced cheeses, enjoyed with a refreshing glass of German beer.

pane toscano
TUSCAN COUNTRY BREAD

In Tuscany bread plays an important part in the food of the region, more so than pasta! This typical country-style loaf is traditionally made without salt to offset the saltiness in the local foods such as salami or prosciutto, as well as the rich cheeses served with them. Traditionally baked in a wood-fired oven, like most Italian breads it is textured with a substantial crust.

INGREDIENTS
MAKES 1 LOAF

2 tsp active dry (1 oz fresh) yeast
pinch of sugar
1 1/4 cups warm water
4 1/2 cups refined durum wheat flour (type 00) flour, plus a little for dusting
4 tbsp good quality olive oil

TO MAKE GNOCCHI

For unusual gnocchi (dumplings) made from left over Tuscan bread, place 8 1/2 cups of bread crumbs in a bowl. Add 1 1/2 cups milk, 1 beaten egg, and 1 cup freshly grated Parmesan.

Add enough white bread flour to form a dough (about 2 1/2 cups), then knead for 5 minutes.

Roll into small balls in the palm of your hands, then poach in boiling water for 2–3 minutes or until they rise to the surface. Rub a buttered ovenproof dish with garlic, transfer the gnocchi to the dish, top with chopped tomatoes and basil, lots of grated cheese and bake for 10 minutes. Drizzle with olive oil and serve.

AND AN ANTIPASTO IDEA

A favorite Italian antipasto is *fettunta*, simply sliced and toasted Tuscan loaf rubbed with garlic and drizzled with good quality olive oil and a sprinkling of sea salt.

---

1 In a small bowl, place the yeast and sugar along with the water, and leave to stand for 10 minutes.

2 Place the flour in a large bowl. Make a well in the center and pour in the yeast liquid along with the olive oil. Bring together to form a soft dough with one hand. Turn out onto a floured surface, knead for 10 minutes until smooth and pliable.

3 Place in a clean, oiled bowl, cover with plastic wrap, and leave in a warm place to rise for 1 to 1 1/2 hours or until doubled in size.

4 Turn out again, knock back to expel the air, and knead again for a further minute. Shape into one large cylinder, place on a lightly dusted baking sheet, cover again, then return to a warm place for further 45 minutes to proof.

5 Preheat the oven to 400°F. Dust liberally with flour, then bake on the center shelf for 35–40 minutes until golden and crusty. Transfer to a cooling rack.

Panini (small breads) or little rolls are made using this dough and are found all over Italy in café bars, filled generously with all manner of cold meats, roasted vegetables, seafood, and salads.

VARIATIONS

For a classic *pane integrate* (whole-wheat bread), simply replace 2 1/2 cups of the flour with an equal amount of whole-wheat flour, proceed as normal.

For *pane salato* (salt bread), add 2 tsp fine sea salt to the basic Tuscan loaf.

pain de campagne
FRENCH SOURDOUGH BREAD

This sourdough starter dough can be prepared a day in advance and kept wrapped in the refrigerator. If doing this, you may omit the second proving. Remove the dough about 3 hours prior to making the bread to let it come to room temperature.

1 For the starter dough, place the flour in a large bowl and make a well in the center. In a small bowl, mix the water with the yeast, then pour it onto the flour, gradually mix together to form a firm dough, using one hand.

2 Turn out the starter dough onto a lightly floured surface, knead for 8–10 minutes, then return to a clean, oiled bowl, cover with plastic wrap or a damp cloth, and leave to rise in a warm place for 4 hours.

3 Turn out the starter dough onto a lightly floured surface again and knock back to expel the air. Place in a bowl, cover again, and proof for further 3 hours.

4 For the basic dough, place the flour in a bowl and make a well in the center. Place water and yeast in a small bowl and leave to stand for 5 minutes. Pour the yeast liquid into the flour, add the salt, the prepared sourdough starter and work well into a smooth pliable dough. Place in a clean bowl, leave to proof for 1 hour.

5 Turn out the dough and knock back to expel the air. Shape into two round loaves, then slightly flatten with your hand. Dust liberally with flour. Using a small sharp knife, cut four slashes on top of each loaf to form a square. Place both loaves on a lightly floured baking sheet, cover, and proof for 1 hour.

6 Preheat the oven to 450°F, or as high as it will go. Place a shallow baking sheet in the base of the oven to heat; throw in some ice cubes to create steam. Place the bread on the top shelf of the oven and bake for 30 minutes until golden. Transfer to a cooling rack.

MAKES 2 LOAVES

FOR THE SOURDOUGH STARTER
scant 1 cup white bread flour
$^1/_4$ cup warm water
1 tsp active dry ($^1/_4$ oz fresh) yeast

FOR THE BASIC DOUGH
4 cups white bread flour
$^1/_2$ cup rye flour
1$^1/_2$ cups warm water
1 tsp active dry ($^1/_2$ oz fresh) yeast
2 tsp fine sea salt

oatmeal bread

Oatmeal is one of Scotland's finest treasures — and it makes a great addition to bread. If possible try to source the organic variety available. This is equally delicious when made with malt flour.

INGREDIENTS
MAKES 2 LOAVES

scant $^3/_4$ cup organic oatmeal, plus a little for dusting
$1^1/_4$ cups milk
$2^1/_4$ cups whole-wheat flour
$2^1/_2$ cups white bread flour
$1^1/_2$ tsp active dry ($^1/_2$ oz fresh) yeast
1 tsp fine sea salt
1 tsp superfine sugar
1 tsp clear honey
$^1/_4$ cup unsalted butter

TROUT IN OATMEAL BREAD CRUMBS

Bread crumbs made of oatmeal bread make a great coating for fresh trout. Simply pass the cleaned trout through seasoned flour, beaten egg, then through the oatmeal crumbs. Sauté in clarified butter until golden and serve with a mustard-flavored tartare sauce.

---

1 Place the oatmeal and the milk in a bowl and leave to soak for 4 hours.

2 Place the flour in a bowl with the yeast, salt, and sugar, and mix well.

3 In a small pan, warm the honey and butter for 1–2 minutes, until melted.

4 Make a well in the center of the flour, pour in the honey and butter, followed by the soaked oatmeal. Bring together with one hand to a soft dough.

5 Turn out the dough onto a floured surface, knead for 8–10 minutes until soft and pliable. Place in a clean bowl, cover with plastic wrap or a damp cloth, and place in a warm place to rise until doubled in size.

6 Turn out the dough and knock back to expel the air. Divide the dough in half and roll out into two rounds. Place on a large baking sheet, spray with water, and dust both liberally with oatmeal. Cover again and return to a warm place to rise for a further hour.

7 Preheat the oven to 425°F. Bake the loaves on the center shelf for 10–12 minutes, then reduce the heat to 350°F and bake for a further 30 minutes or until cooked and golden. Transfer loaves to a cooling rack.

VARIATION

Make a tasty granola-crusted bread — after the first rising divide the dough into 2 loaves and flatten them lightly, then brush the loaves with warm honey, sprinkle liberally with granola. Cover with a damp cloth, set to proof for a further hour, then bake as before and serve, drizzled with warm honey, straight from the oven.

classic baguette

For me the baguette is *the* rustic loaf. To recreate the baguette at home a very hot oven and steam is needed to give that crusty texture. This bread needs to be started the day before.

INGREDIENTS
MAKES 1 LOAF

2²/₃ cups white bread flour
1³/₄ cups all-purpose flour, preferably French (type 55 flour)
2 tsp fine sea salt
1½ tsp active dry (½ oz fresh) yeast
1¼ cups warm water

SCALLOPS WITH A HAZELNUT-BREAD CRUMB CRUST

For a great fresh tasting fish dish using scallops topped with hazelnut crust, simply place some French bread in a blender or food processor with equal amounts of peeled hazelnuts and blitz to a coarse crumb.

Transfer to a bowl, add some crushed garlic, grated lemon zest, and some chopped fresh cilantro. Finally add enough melted butter to give it a sloppy consistency.

Clean the scallops, return to their shell, season them, then top liberally with the hazelnut crust. Cook under a hot broiler for 3–4 minutes and serve. Simplicity itself!

GARLIC BREAD

When the baguette is old and stale, I make garlic bread with it: cut the loaf in slices, not cutting right through to the base. Fill the cuts with garlic butter and wrap in foil, bake for 10–15 minutes in the oven preheated to 375°F, and serve.

---

1 Firstly prepare a starter, following the sponge method (see page 8). Sift the flours and salt together in a large bowl. In another large bowl, mix the yeast with the water, stir to dissolve, and leave to stand for 10 minutes.

2 Beat in half the flour mix to make a thick batter. Cover with plastic wrap, leave at room temperature for 4 hours or until nearly doubled in size. During this time the batter will collapse.

3 Add the rest of the flour to the batter, beating it in with one hand. Turn out onto a floured surface, knead for 8–10 minutes to form a moist dough. Place in a clean bowl and leave to rest in a warm place, covered for 1 hour.

4 Turn out the dough onto a lightly floured surface, knock back to expel the air and roll into a baguette shape, or alternatively, place in a classic baguette frame or *banneton* and leave to proof for a further hour.

5 Preheat the oven to 450°F or maximum heat, placing a baking tray filled with boiling water in the base of the oven.

6 Make 5–6 slashes across the loaf in long diagonal slits. Bake on the top shelf of the oven for 25–30 minutes until golden and crusty. Transfer to a cooling rack. Baguette is best eaten on the day it is made.

Classic baguettes are illustrated on the endpapers of the book.

VARIATIONS

In France baguettes are often made in varying sizes. *Ficelles* (string) are exactly that, a long, thin variation on the basic recipe.

For herb-flavored baguettes, simply add chopped herbs to the basic flour and proceed as normal.

I also love to make mini baguette rolls (seen right) shaped with pointed ends. They not only look great but are wonderfully crisp.

potted saffron brioche

Rich and buttery, brioche is the pinnacle of sweet bread to my mind, wonderful for breakfast with lashings of good butter. The use of small flowerpots makes a nice presentation as well as baking receptacle, but they need preparing before baking (see note below).

1 Heat the milk with the saffron for 2 minutes, cool to lukewarm, then add the yeast.

2 Place the flour and salt in a large bowl, make a well in the center. Add the saffron yeast mixture to the flour, then the eggs and mix together with one hand to form a soft dough. With a wooden spoon, beat the dough for 3–4 minutes until smooth.

3 In a separate bowl, cream the butter and sugar together until light and fluffy, then beat gradually into the dough a little at a time until amalgamated. Beat until smooth and pliable.

4 Cover the bowl with plastic wrap or a damp cloth, leave to rise in a warm place for $1\frac{1}{2}$ hours or until doubled in size. Lightly knock back the dough, cover with plastic wrap, and place in the refrigerator overnight. Overnight the dough will stiffen.

5 Turn the dough out onto a lightly floured surface and divide into 15 small balls, about 2 oz each, and place in the greased, prepared flowerpots lined with parchment paper. Place the molds on a large baking sheet, cover and leave in a warm place to rise again for 1 hour.

6 Preheat the oven to 400°F. Brush the glaze over the top of the brioches. Bake for 10–12 minutes until golden brown. Transfer to a cooling rack.

NOTE

To prepare flowerpots for baking, wipe them out thoroughly, oil them inside and out, and place in an oven set at 275°F to proof for 30 minutes. Remove and cool, then do the same process a further 2 times. This will strengthen the molds and stop them from cracking during cooking.

VARIATIONS

Of course, this brioche dough can be cooked in a loaf-pan form, or shaped into small rolls. I love the addition of 3 tbsp finely chopped crystallized ginger to the flour at the start of preparation, then when cooked, sliced, and lightly toasted, top with lots of butter oozing over the sweet bread.

INGREDIENTS
MAKES 15 SMALL POTS

$\frac{1}{3}$ cup warm milk
good pinch of saffron powder
$1\frac{1}{2}$ tsp active dry ($\frac{1}{2}$ oz fresh) yeast
3 cups white bread flour
$\frac{1}{2}$ tsp fine sea salt
3 eggs
$\frac{3}{4}$ cup unsalted butter, softened
2 tbs superfine sugar
1 egg yolk mixed with 1 tbsp milk, to glaze

BRIOCHE AND ORANGE PUDDING

For a delicious brioche, mascarpone and orange pudding, heat 300ml ($1\frac{1}{4}$ cups) of milk in a pan, add 100g ($3\frac{1}{2}$ oz) saffron brioche cubes and 150g ($\frac{2}{3}$ cup) mascarpone cheese, leave to stand.

When cold, add 4 lightly beaten eggs, zest of 1 orange, then pour into 4 buttered large ramekins and bake for 25 minutes until golden, keeping them light and moist in the center. Serve with cream and fresh fruit.

SALMON WITH A CRUMB CRUST

Saffron brioche crumbs, mixed with melted butter and herbs, make a great crust for salmon. Seal the seasoned salmon fillet in butter, then cool. Top with a fine crust of the bread crumbs, place on a grill (broiler) pan and place under the grill (broiler) until the salmon is cooked and the saffron crumbs just golden brown and crispy.

pumpkin and green olive bread

Here is one of my favorite olive breads flavored with sweet pumpkin and aromatic oregano. Traditionally Greek breads are made with olive oil, but this one uses butter. It is great with mezze.

1 Preheat the oven to 375°F. Line a small roasting pan with lightly greased foil, add the pumpkin, drizzle over the olive oil, and bake for 40 minutes or until the pumpkin is very soft. Pass the flesh through a strainer, leave to go cold.

2 Meanwhile, sift flour and salt in a large bowl, rub in the chilled butter to resemble coarse bread crumbs.

3 Mix the yeast with the sugar, add the warmed milk, and leave for 5 minutes. Add to the flour, along with the eggs, pumpkin purée, oregano, then bring to a soft dough using one hand, adding a little more milk if necessary.

4 Turn out onto a floured surface, knead for 10 minutes or until the dough is soft and pliable. Place in a lightly oiled bowl, cover with plastic wrap, leave to rise in a warm place for 1 hour or until doubled in volume.

5 Turn out the dough again, knock back to expel the air. Add the olives and work quickly into the dough. Shape into two equal-sized cylinder loaves, brush or spray with a little water, scatter the pumpkin seeds over, and place on a large, oiled baking sheet. Cover again and leave to rise for 45 minutes.

6 Increase the oven heat to 400°F. Brush the loaves with beaten egg to glaze. Bake on the center shelf of the oven, for 35–40 minutes until golden and cooked. Transfer to a cooling rack.

INGREDIENTS
MAKES 2 LOAVES

10 oz pumpkin or squash, peeled, cut into large wedges

2 tbsp olive oil

6 cups white bread flour

1 tbsp fine sea salt

$^1/_4$ cup unsalted butter, chilled, cut into small pieces

$1^1/_2$ tsp active dry ($^1/_2$ oz fresh) yeast

2 tsp superfine sugar

$1^1/_4$ cups warm milk

2 eggs, plus a little eggwash for glazing

1 tbsp chopped fresh oregano

$^3/_4$ cup green olives, pitted, roughly chopped

3 tbsp pumpkin seeds

skillet chestnut cornbread with chorizo

I love cornbread. It is not only crumbly in texture, delicious in taste, but its versatility knows no bounds. This one is slightly spiced with sausage and with the addition of chestnuts. Great served with chili con carne or as part of a bread selection for brunch.

1   Preheat the oven to 375°F. Heat a non-stick skillet over a moderate heat, add the chorizo and chestnuts, and cook for 2–3 minutes until golden, remove and allow to cool.

2   Combine the flour, polenta, salt, baking powder, and sugar in a mixing bowl; make a well in the center. Add the eggs, butter, and milk, and mix well to form a smooth batter. Stir in the chorizo, chestnuts, and ³/₄ cup of the grated cheese.

3   Heat a deep 8 inch ovenproof skillet lightly greased with oil. Pour in the mix and smooth the surface. Bake for 20 minutes. Remove from the oven, sprinkle the remaining cheese over the center of the bread and return to the oven for a further 5 minutes. Remove and allow to cool before turning out, cutting into wedges to serve.

INGREDIENTS
MAKES 1 LOAF

3 oz chorizo sausage, finely diced
3 oz cooked chestnuts, finely chopped
1¹/₄ cups all-purpose flour
1¹/₄ cups fine cornmeal
pinch of fine sea salt
4 tsp baking powder
¹/₄ cup superfine sugar
2 eggs, beaten
2 tbsp unsalted butter, melted
1¹/₄ cups milk
scant 1 cup finely grated Cheddar cheese
oil for greasing

THANKSGIVING CORNBREAD STUFFING

Cornbread is often made into stuffing to serve on Thanksgiving with the traditional turkey. Here is my favorite cornbread stuffing recipe with apple and pecan nuts.

Heat ¹/₄ cup butter in a large pan, add 2 finely chopped onions along with 2 tbsp chopped fresh sage or rosemary, and cook until softened. Add 2 apples, peeled, cored, and chopped, and cook for 5 minutes or until softened.

Add 8¹/₂ cups crumbled cornbread and 1 cup chopped pecans, cook over a low heat until softened and well combined. Cool, then stir in 2 eggs, and season to taste. Use to stuff turkey or cook in the oven separately.

herb breads

florentine

PARMESAN AND ROSEMARY BREAD

I love this simple cheese bread I first
tasted in Naples. The chef kindly gave
me the recipe in Italian! It is best
eaten fresh – warm from the oven.

INGREDIENTS

MAKES 2 LONG BATONS

4$\frac{1}{2}$ cups white bread flour
1 cup freshly grated Parmigiano Reggiano cheese, plus
a little extra for dusting
1$\frac{1}{2}$ tsp active dry ($\frac{1}{2}$ oz fresh) yeast
1 tsp fine sea salt
1 large egg, beaten
3 tbsp virgin olive oil
1 cup warm water
2 tbsp chopped fresh rosemary, plus 2 rosemary sprigs

1 Place the flour, cheese, dried yeast and salt in a large bowl.

2 Add the egg and olive oil and, using one hand, bring together with the water to form a dough.

3 Turn out onto a floured surface and knead for 5–10 minutes to a smooth, elastic, and pliable dough. Add the rosemary and mix well. Place in a lightly oiled bowl, cover with plastic wrap or a damp cloth and leave to rise in a warm place for 45 minutes or until doubled in size.

4 Turn out the dough again onto a floured surface and knock back to expel the air.

5 Preheat the oven to 350°F. Lightly grease a baking sheet with a little oil. Shape the dough into 2 long batons, slash a cut down center of each with a sharp knife, and place on the baking sheet. Cover with a damp cloth, return to a warm place to rise again for 30 minutes or until doubled in size.

6 Spray or brush with a little water, dust lightly with the Parmesan and arrange the rosemary sprigs down the center of each loaf. Bake on the center shelf, about 30–35 minutes or until the bread is golden. Transfer to a cooling rack.

stuffed greek rolls

The filling for these little stuffed rolls
is really down to personal choice – by
using mozzarella and sundried
tomatoes you can add an Italian touch.

INGREDIENTS

MAKES 4 4-ROLL LOAVES

5$\frac{1}{4}$ cups refined durum wheat flour (type 00) flour
1$\frac{1}{2}$ tsp active dry ($\frac{3}{4}$ oz fresh) yeast
1 tsp fine sea salt
2 tbsp olive oil
1$\frac{1}{4}$ cups warm water

FOR THE FILLING
4 oz Greek feta cheese, crumbled
$\frac{1}{2}$ cup sundried tomatoes, chopped
2 large red bell peppers, roasted, chopped
15 black olives, pitted, halved
1 tsp chopped fresh oregano

1 Sift the flour in a large mixing bowl, add the yeast and salt. Make a well in the center, add the oil, gradually add the water, and using one hand, bring together to a soft dough. Turn out the dough on a lightly floured surface, knead for half a minute until soft.

2 Return to the bowl, cover with plastic wrap and place in a warm place to proof for 1 to 1$\frac{1}{2}$ hours or until doubled in size. Meanwhile, mix all the filling ingredients together.

3 Turn out the dough again, knock back to expel the air and knead to a smooth pliable dough. Divide the dough into 16 equal size rolls. Flatten by hand, or using a floured rolling pin, to roll each piece to a 4 inch circle. Place a small pile of the filling in the center of each circle, then fold over each piece of dough to form an oval and pinch the seams together.

4 Arrange the rolls close together on floured large baking sheets, overlapping the points to make 4 x 4-roll loaves. Dust liberally with flour, cover with a cloth, and leave to rise again in a warm place for 25 minutes or until doubled in size.

5 Preheat the oven to 425°F. Place the baking sheets on the center shelf of the oven and bake for 15 minutes until golden. Transfer to a cooling rack.

polenta, basil, and roasted-tomato bread

In my eyes, whether made into a loaf or individual rolls, this Italian staple is great served with just about anything!

INGREDIENTS
MAKES 3 SMALL LOAVES

1³/₄ cups water
³/₄ cup polenta (fine cornmeal)
3¹/₂ cups white bread flour
2 tsp fine sea salt
1 tsp active dry (¹/₃ oz fresh) yeast
1 tsp sugar
4 tbsp milk
³/₄ cup sundried tomatoes in oil, drained well, chopped
1 tbsp prepared pesto
mix of flour and polenta for dusting

TOMATOES COOKED WITH A CRUMB CRUST

Make fine bread crumbs from the polenta bread and mix in a bowl with melted butter and crushed garlic, and chopped red chilli.

Halve some small tomatoes horizontally, place on a baking sheet. Season liberally with salt, pepper, pinch of sugar, then top with the bread crumbs.

Place the sheet under a hot preheated broiler to brown the crumbs and cook the tomatoes.

Serve with spaghetti, tossed with seasoning and olive oil, and sprinkled with fresh basil.

ROMAN STYLE KEBABS

For Roman style kebabs, remove crusts from the loaf, cut into ¹/₄ inch slices, then each slice into 2 inch squares. Brush with butter or olive oil, then skewer onto wooden skewers alternating with slices of mozzarella and sliced tomatoes. Broil until golden and the cheese is melting, drizzle with pesto, and serve.

---

1 Bring 1 cup of the water to a boil, scatter in the polenta, and beat with a wooden spoon until smooth, about 4–5 minutes, remove from the heat and cool.

2 Place the flour in a large mixing bowl with the salt.

3 In a small bowl, mix the yeast with the sugar and milk, leave for 5 minutes.

4 Add the polenta mixture to the flour, rub in with your fingers to amalgamate. Make a well in the center, pour in the yeast liquid, add the chopped tomatoes, and bring together with the remaining water to form a soft pliable dough.

5 Turn out onto a floured surface, knead for 8–10 minutes and return to the bowl. Cover with plastic wrap and leave in a warm place to proof for 1 hour or until almost double in size.

6 Preheat the oven to 400°F. Turn the dough out onto a floured table again and knock back to expel the air. Lightly work in the pesto to give a marbled appearance and shape into 3 small oval loaves. Place on a lightly dusted baking sheet, leaving space between them. Dust with the flour and polenta mix. Cover with a cloth and leave in warm place to rise again for further 45 minutes.

7 Bake on the center shelf for 25–30 minutes until golden. Transfer to a cooling rack before eating.

VARIATIONS

There are some great-tasting sundried peppers now on the market; use them instead of the tomatoes in this recipe.

1 Place half the flour, and the salt in a large mixing bowl.

2 Place the water, sugar, and yeast in a jug, and stir to dissolve. Add to the flour and mix to a smooth soft dough. Place in a clean bowl, cover with plastic wrap and leave to proof in a warm place for 45 minutes.

3 Mix the egg, cheese, olive oil, and dill together and add to the dough. Sprinkle in the remaining flour and knead to a pliable dough, smooth and elastic. Place in an oiled bowl, cover again and proof for 1½ hours, until doubled in size.

4 Turn out the dough onto a floured surface and knock back to expel air. Shape into 2 well greased 1 lb loaf pans, and place on a baking sheet. Proof once again in a warm place for a further 30 minutes.

5 Preheat the oven to 375°F. Brush the loaves with the egg and yogurt then bake on the center shelf for 45 minutes until golden. Transfer to a cooling rack.

VARIATIONS

Make into small rolls – they are great filled with smoked salmon or other smoked fish with horseradish/dill crème fraîche.

dill and curd cheese bread

In this Norwegian recipe the soft curd cheese adds a little acidity to the bread. It is wonderful served with smoked fish such as smoked salmon.

INGREDIENTS
MAKES 2 LOAVES

4 cups white bread flour
1 tsp fine sea salt
1 cup warm water
1 tbsp superfine sugar
1 tsp active dry yeast
1 egg, lightly beaten
⅓ cup soft curd cheese (i.e ricotta, cottage cheese)
2 tbsp olive oil
4 tbsp chopped fresh dill
1 egg yolk mixed with 3 tbsp plain yogurt

1 Place the flour, salt, curry powder, cumin, cardamom, and turmeric in a bowl.

2 In a small bowl blend the yeast with the warm water until liquid, then add to the flour. Mix it well by hand adding more water if necessary until a soft dough is formed.

3 Turn out the dough onto a lightly floured surface and knead for 5–10 minutes until smooth and elastic. Place the dough into a clean bowl, cover with plastic wrap or a damp cloth, and leave to proof in a warm place until the dough has doubled in size.

4 Preheat the oven to 425°F. Turn out the dough onto lightly floured surface and knock back to expel the air.

5 Shape the dough into 2 x 6 inch rounds, place on a baking sheet, and proof again for a further 40 minutes until doubled in size.

6 Spray or brush with water, then stud the bread evenly with the curry leaves. Scatter the ajwain seeds over and bake on the center shelf for 25–30 minutes until cooked. Transfer to a cooling rack.

Pan-Asian Cob is illustrated on page 2.

pan-asian cob

I created this Pan-Asian bread one day with some soft white loaf base, some Asian spices, and a creative mind! It is full of flavor and always popular.

INGREDIENTS
MAKES 2 LOAVES

4½ cups white bread flour, plus a little
  extra for dusting
2 tsp fine sea salt
1 tsp mild curry powder
½ tsp ground cumin
½ tsp ground cardamom
¼ tsp ground turmeric
1½ tsp active dry (¾ oz fresh) yeast
1⅓ cups warm water
8–10 fresh curry leaves
1 tsp ajwain seeds

roast garlic—rosemary bâtard

If you've got a taste for garlic bread, then you'll love this one, in which the garlic is roasted until lightly caramelized with added fresh rosemary before being incorporated within the dough. Bâtard (or bastard) is a French peasant-style loaf, misshapen in style, hence its name.

INGREDIENTS
MAKES 2 LOAVES

$3\frac{1}{2}$ oz (about 20) garlic cloves, unpeeled
2 tbsp olive oil
4 tbsp chopped fresh rosemary
$4\frac{1}{2}$ cups white bread flour plus a little extra for dusting
2 tsp fine sea salt
$1\frac{1}{2}$ tsp active dry yeast
$1\frac{1}{4}$ cups warm water

1 Preheat the oven to 400°F. Place the garlic in a baking pan, drizzle the oil over, and roast for 30 minutes until the garlic is very soft and caramelized. When warm, pop the garlic out of its skin between your fingers into a bowl. Mash the garlic lightly with a fork, add the rosemary and place on one side.

2 Place the flour and salt in a large mixing bowl with the yeast, add most of the water and bring together with one hand, adding more water if necessary, to make a soft pliable dough.

3 Turn out the dough and add the garlic and rosemary mix; knead for 8–10 minutes until smooth and elastic. Return to the bowl, cover with plastic wrap and leave in warm place to rise for 1 hour or until doubled in size.

4 Turn out the dough again, knock back to expel air, then knead for a further 2 minutes. Shape into 2 oval baton shapes about 10 inches in length. Transfer to a baking sheet, dust with a little flour and lightly cover with a cloth; leave to proof in a warm place for a further 30 minutes.

5 Using a sharp knife, make some $\frac{1}{4}$ inch deep slits over the surface of the loaves. Bake on the top shelf of the oven for 25–30 minutes, until the bread is golden or sounds hollow when the bottom is tapped. Transfer to a cooling wire to cool.

ONION SOUP

I particularly like this bread topped with Gruyère cheese, served on a classical onion-soup base.

MUSHROOM AND BREAD OMELET

Heat a small omelet pan or non-stick skillet with a little olive oil. Throw in some sliced mushrooms, preferably wild, along with some garlic and chopped shallots. Cook until golden, add cubes of bâtard bread, and toss with the mushrooms. Finally add some roughly chopped flat-leaf parsley and pour over 3 beaten eggs.

Using a fork, lightly bring the mix together until the eggs are just set. Turn out onto a plate and serve – delicious!

potato, thyme, and goat cheese pavé

One of my personal favorites: I love potatoes and goat cheese so it seemed obvious to create a loaf with these in mind. The goat cheese must be a matured variety for the best flavor possible. Pavé is French for cobblestone, which reflects the shape of the loaf.

1 Place the flour in a large bowl, rub in the butter to resemble coarse bread crumbs. In a small bowl, mix half the milk or water, the yeast, and sugar and leave to stand for 10 minutes until frothy.

2 Make a well in the center of the flour, pour in the yeast liquid and the remaining milk or water. Add the warm mashed potato, salt, egg, and grated cheese and bring together with one hand to form a dough.

3 Turn out the dough on a lightly floured surface and knead it for 8–10 minutes until smooth and elastic. Place the dough in a clean, lightly oiled bowl, covered with plastic wrap, and leave in a warm place for 1 hour or until doubled in size.

4 Turn out the dough again and knock back to expel the air. Add the fresh thyme and mix well. Shape into a rectangular loaf and place on a greased baking sheet. Cover with a damp cloth and return to a warm place to rise for a further 40–45 minutes or until doubled in size.

5 Preheat the oven to 400°F. Using a sharp knife, score deep slits in a criss-cross fashion on the top of the bread. Brush the loaf lightly all over with extra beaten egg (or spray with water and dust with flour for a crustier loaf), then bake on a center shelf for 25–30 minutes until golden. Check to see if bread is cooked before transferring to a cooling rack. Cut into squares to serve.

INGREDIENTS
MAKES 1 LOAF

$4^{1}/_2$ cups white bread flour
$^{1}/_4$ cup unsalted butter, chilled, cut into small cubes
1 cup plus 2 tbsp warm milk or water
$1^{1}/_2$ tsp active dry ($^{3}/_4$ oz fresh) yeast
1 tsp sugar
1 cup plain mashed potato, warm (no added cream or butter)
1 tsp fine sea salt
1 egg, beaten
$^{2}/_3$ cup mature goat cheese, grated
1 tbsp fresh thyme leaves

STUFFING FOR CHICKEN OR LAMB

Use any leftover bread, made into bread crumbs, to make a great stuffing for roast chicken or roast lamb.

Heat 2 tbsp unsalted butter in a large skillet and when hot add 1 finely chopped onion and $^{3}/_4$ cup chopped walnuts and cook until lightly golden. Add $4^{1}/_2$ cups potato, thyme and goat cheese bread crumbs, $^{1}/_4$ cup unsalted butter, increase the heat and cook until the bread crumbs are golden and crispy.

VARIATIONS

Try replacing the goat cheese with mature Cheddar, half added to the flour at the initial stages of making the dough and the remainder sprinkled on top before baking.

flatbreads and sticks

naan

PUNJABI FLATBREAD

Naan is traditionally charred in a clay oven called a tandoor and this gives the most authentic flavor. Dry frying in a large non-stick pan or even a wok is the best way to cook them at home.

INGREDIENTS
MAKES 8

1$\frac{1}{2}$ tsp active dry ($\frac{3}{4}$ oz fresh) yeast
about $\frac{3}{4}$ cup warm milk or water
4$\frac{1}{2}$ cups white bread flour
5 tbsp plain yogurt
1 tsp cumin seeds or 2 tsp white sesame seeds
1 tsp baking powder
1 tsp fine sea salt
2 tbsp ghee or unsalted butter, melted
2 tbsp chopped fresh cilantro (optional)

1 Dissolve the yeast with the warm milk or water in a large bowl, leave to stand for 5 minutes. Whisk in half the flour, cover, and leave to stand for 15 minutes in a warm place to get a simple starter going.

2 Add the remaining flour, the yogurt, cumin, baking powder, and salt and bring together with one hand to form a soft dough.

3 Add half the ghee or melted butter, knead for 8–10 minutes to form a soft pliable dough. Place in a lightly oiled bowl, cover with plastic wrap, and leave in a warm place for 45 minutes or until doubled in size.

4 Turn out onto a lightly floured surface, knock back to expel the air. Knock back again, then divide the dough into 8 equal size balls, and roll out with a little flour to an oval or round shape, about 1$\frac{1}{4}$ inch thick. Brush with the remaining ghee or butter.

5 Cook in a hot non-stick pan for 1–2 minutes on each side until golden and puffed up. Remove and keep warm while you cook the remaining naans the same way. Sprinkle with cilantro, if using, and serve.

parathas

WHOLE-WHEAT GRIDDLE BREAD

These unleavened breads are very popular in India, especially made for special occasions and religious festivals. You can alter the flavor by adding various herbs and spices.

INGREDIENTS
MAKES 6

1$\frac{1}{4}$ cups all-purpose flour, plus a little extra for kneading
$\frac{2}{3}$ cup whole-wheat flour
pinch of salt
12 lovage seeds, lightly crushed (optional)
$\frac{1}{2}$ cup ghee or clarified butter, melted
$\frac{1}{4}$ cup milk mixed with $\frac{1}{4}$ cup water

1 Sift the flours with a pinch of salt into a large bowl and add the lovage seeds, if using. Add 2 tbsp of the ghee or clarified butter, rub it into the flour until it resembles coarse bread crumbs.

2 Add the milk and water to make a soft and pliable dough, then turn out onto the work surface and knead until smooth. Cover the dough with plastic wrap and set aside for 2 hours.

3 Divide the dough into 6 and roll out to make 6 perfect circles, about 7 inches across, and then brush them with a little melted ghee or clarified butter. Fold the circles in half, then fold again to make quarters. Roll them out again to their former size.

4 Brush them with melted ghee again and repeat the folding process. Do this twice more.

5 Cook the parathas one by one on a hot lightly buttered griddle or heavy-based skillet until they are pale brown and mottled. Turn them over and cook on the other side. Keep them warm in foil as you work. These parathas can be made a couple of days in advance, refrigerated, and reheated under a hot grill when needed.

grissini

FLAVORED ITALIAN BREADSTICKS

These Italian breadsticks have been served in trattoria all over Italy for many years, they are irresistible and simple to prepare — purchased varieties are not in the same league. They are also excellent served with dips for pre-dinner nibbles with drinks.

1   Place the flour, salt, yeast, and both oils in a bowl, mix together. Gradually add the water and mix with one hand to pull the dough together.

2   Turn out the dough onto a lightly floured surface and knead for 8–10 minutes until the dough is smooth and pliable. Roll out the dough on a lightly floured surface into a rectangle 6 x 8 inches, by $\frac{1}{2}$ inch thick.

3   Brush with olive oil, cover with plastic wrap or a damp cloth, leave to rise in a warm place for 30–45 minutes or until doubled in size.

4   Preheat the oven to 400°F. Using a ruler as a guide, cut off thin stripes with a sharp knife. Roll each strip back and forth in sesame seeds, to make long thin sticks. (Do not use extra flour when rolling them out as too much hinders the rolling process.) Place on a baking sheet, spaced well apart.

5   Place in the oven on a center shelf for 15–20 minutes then transfer to a cooling wire to cool. Leave to become dry and crisp before eating.

INGREDIENTS
MAKES 20–24 STICKS

2$\frac{1}{4}$ cups white bread flour
$\frac{1}{2}$ tsp fine sea salt
1 tsp active dry ($\frac{1}{3}$ oz fresh) yeast
1 tbsp olive oil, plus a little for brushing
1 tbsp sesame oil
$\frac{2}{3}$ cup warm water
sesame seeds for coating

FINGER FOOD IDEA

These sticks make great hors d'oeuvres to serve with drinks. Wrap the cooked grissini with cured meat such as prosciutto or bresaola, then served with a creamy ricotta and chive dip for dunking.

VARIATIONS

These breadsticks are so versatile, here are some variations on the theme:

Add $\frac{1}{2}$ cup freshly grated Parmesan to the flour;

Flavor them with your favorite herb — thyme and rosemary are particularly good — or spice them up with curry powder, paprika, or ground cumin;

Scatter some coarse sea salt over before baking;

Vary the exterior by using poppy seeds or other seeds, such as flax or hemp.

1   Sift the flour and salt in a large bowl, add the yeast.

2   Mix the warm water with ¼ cup of the olive oil, the garlic, ginger, and cilantro. Pour onto the flour and mix to form a soft dough; turn out onto a lightly floured surface, then knead until smooth and elastic, about 2–3 minutes.

3   Place in a lightly oiled bowl, cover with plastic wrap, and leave to rise in a warm place for 1 to 1½ hours or until doubled in size.

4   Preheat the oven to 400°F. Turn out the dough and knock back to expel the air, knead for 2 minutes.

5   Roll out the dough to an oblong, about 1 inch thick. Place in a well greased 10 x 12 inch baking pan. Make indentations at 1 inch intervals all over the dough with floured fingers.

6   Brush over the remaining olive oil, then place in the oven for 25–30 minutes until golden in color and spongy in texture.

7   Mix together the sweet chili sauce and vegetable oil in a bowl, then brush it all over the surface of the bread two or three times while warm. Remove the bread from the pan, serve warm or at room temperature.

asian-style focaccia

This is my idea of an Asian-style *focaccia* — flavor packed with all the ingredients I adore: ginger, fresh cilantro and sweet chilli.

INGREDIENTS
MAKES 1 BREAD

6 cups white bread flour
1 tbsp fine sea salt
1½ tsp active dry yeast
2 cups warm water
⅓ cup olive oil
1 garlic clove, crushed
3 tbsp Japanese pink pickled ginger, roughly chopped or 2 tbsp grated root ginger
4 tbsp chopped fresh cilantro
¼ cup good quality sweet chili sauce
2 tbsp vegetable oil

1   Dissolve the yeast and sugar in half the water. Sift the flour into a bowl, add salt, pour in the dissolved yeast, and stir well. Add the remaining water and bring to a soft dough using one hand. Knead until smooth and pliable, 8–10 minutes. Place the dough in a clean lightly oiled bowl, cover with plastic wrap, leave in a warm place for 1 hour or until doubled in size.

2   Turn out the dough, knock back to expel the air, knead again for 2 minutes. Using a floured rolling pin, roll out the dough to about ⅛–¼ inch thick. With a 3 inch cookie cutter, cut out 16–20 rounds; chill in the refrigerator on a tray.

3   For the filling, heat the olive oil in a pan, add the shallot, garlic, and chorizo, and cook until golden, about 5 minutes. Add the tomatoes, reduce the heat, and cook until thick. Cool and add the cilantro. Preheat the oven to 425°F. Place a spoonful of filling in the center of half of the dough rounds. Brush the edge with a little water, then top the filling with the remaining rounds, pushing down to seal the edges.

4   Brush the egg yolk and olive oil mixture over the pillows. Place on a greased baking sheet and bake for 10–12 minutes until golden and cooked. Leave to cool slightly and serve warm.

turkish stuffed pillow bread

These little cheese-filled bread pillows are made with a *pide* (Turkish flatbread) dough and baked until golden.

MAKES 8–10

FOR THE DOUGH
1½ tsp active dry (¾ oz fresh) yeast
pinch of sugar
1 cup plus 2 tbsp warm water
4½ cups all purpose flour
1 tsp fine sea salt
1 egg yolk mixed with 1 tbsp olive oil

FOR THE FILLING
2 tbsp olive oil
1 shallot, chopped
1 garlic clove, crushed
3 oz chorizo sausage, cut into small dice
14 oz canned tomatoes, drained, chopped
2 tbsp chopped fresh cilantro

See illustration page 5.

pane carasau

SARDINIAN PARCHMENT BREAD

These thin crispy bread sheets originate from Sardinia, but are eaten all over Italy. Sometimes better known as *carta di musica* (music sheets) *pane carasau* was once a specialty of the shepherds on the island, because once baked they stay fresh for a long period of time.

1 Preheat the oven to 425°F. Place the flour, semolina flour, and salt in a large bowl. Slowly add the water, stirring to form a soft dough. Work the dough into a ball for about 2 minutes.

2 Turn out onto a lightly floured surface, knead for a further minute until the dough is firm and pliable and not sticky. Divide the dough into 12 evenly sized balls. Flatten each ball to about 1 inch in thickness.

3 Roll out the dough as thinly as possible into neat rounds – the dough should almost be transparent when held up to the light.

4 Place 1 sheet a large ungreased baking sheet and place in the oven until golden, about 3–4 minutes (baking time will also depend on the amount of breads baked at one time).

5 Turn the sheets over using kitchen tongs, bake other side for 3–4 minutes. Transfer to a cooling rack. These will keep for two weeks stored in an airtight container. Reheat in the oven for 2 minutes and they will be as good as fresh.

VARIATIONS

Top the bread before baking with some olive oil heated and infused with garlic and fresh rosemary. Brush over the sheets and bake as normal.

Brush the bread liberally with pesto and sprinkle generously with fresh Parmigiano Reggiano cheese after cooling. Place under a hot broiler just to melt the cheese and serve.

INGREDIENTS
MAKES 12 SHEETS

2 cups white bread flour
1 cup semolina flour
$\frac{1}{2}$ tsp fine sea salt
1 cup plus 2 tbsp water

PANE FRATTAU

Another regional specialty from Sardinia using this bread is *pane frattau*.

For one person, place 1 sheet of cooked *pane carasau* in a deep dish. Spoon over 3 tbsp of hot water and allow the bread to soften and become pliable, about 2–3 minutes.

Meanwhile fry an egg in a non-stick pan with 2 tbsp olive oil, spoon 4 tbsp of tomato passata (canned tomato purée) over the soaked bread, then transfer to a smaller plate.

Top with the fried egg, sprinkle some freshly grated *pecorino sardo* cheese over, and serve. Drizzle over a little truffle oil as well if you like the idea!

potato flatbread pizza with wild mushrooms and Fontina

This potato flatbread is actually a pizza-style dough made from baked or mashed potatoes with butter. The resulting dough is light and makes a great base for a variety of toppings (see below). Here sautéed wild mushrooms and Fontina cheese are my preferred choice.

1 Preheat the oven to 400°F. Wrap the potatoes in foil and bake for 1 hour or until soft. Remove from the foil and leave until cool enough to handle, then remove the skins. Push the skinned potato through a ricer, then measure the potato, you will need 1 cup in total.

2 Place the potato in a large bowl, add the butter, flour, yeast, and sugar, and mix thoroughly. Mix the warm milk into the potato mixture and combine to form a dough. Turn out onto a floured work surface and knead for 5–8 minutes until smooth and elastic.

3 Place in a lightly oiled bowl, cover with plastic wrap and leave in a warm place for 1 hour or until doubled in size.

4 Turn out the dough and knock back, to expel the air. Roll out the dough round with a rolling pin to fit a 10 inch pizza tray or baking sheet.

5 For the topping, heat the butter in a skillet, add the shallot and garlic, and cook for 2 minutes. Add the mushrooms and sauté for 2–3 minutes until cooked and golden. Season to taste. Reheat the oven to 400°F.

6 Distribute the potatoes along with the mushrooms evenly over the pizza base and sprinkle the shaved Fontina over. Cook for 20–25 minutes until golden and puffed up. Drizzle the olive oil over and serve straight from the oven, cut into wedges.

MAKES 2 10-INCH PIZZAS

FOR THE PIZZA
2 medium baking potatoes
2 tbsp soft butter
2 cups all-purpose flour
$1^{1}/_{2}$ tsp active dry yeast
1 tsp sugar
$^{2}/_{3}$ cup warm milk

FOR THE TOPPING
$^{1}/_{4}$ cup unsalted butter
1 shallot, finely chopped
1 garlic clove, crushed
12 oz mixed wild mushrooms
salt and freshly cracked black pepper
14 oz new potatoes (preferably purple variety), cooked, peeled, thinly sliced
$3^{1}/_{2}$ oz Fontina cheese, thinly shaved
2 tbsp olive oil

VARIATIONS

Here is a selection of other topping ideas –

Spiced tomatoes with red onion and arugula

Broiled vegetables with grated mozzarella

Marinated artichokes, mushrooms and crumbled goat cheese.

schiacciata with vine grapes

Schiacciata is a Tuscan bread, similar to the better-known *focaccia*. Originally cooked in the ashes of the fire, the name means "squashed," an indication of its flattish shape. Tuscans simply love it brushed with good quality olive oil.

1 Sift the flour into a large bowl and add the salt. If using fresh yeast, warm the wine and dissolve the yeast in it. If using active dry yeast, add it to the flour, and leave to stand for 5 minutes.

2 Make a well in the center of the flour and add the wine and the oil. Gradually add the water to form a soft dough, adding a little extra flour if necessary. Turn out the dough onto a lightly floured surface, knead for 1–2 minutes until soft and pliable.

3 Return to the bowl, cover with plastic wrap, and leave in a warm place to proof and rise for 45 minutes to 1 hour or until doubled in size.

4 Turn out the dough on a lightly floured surface, knead for 5 minutes to knock back and expel the air. Divide the dough into 12 equal size balls and roll out using a rolling pin to about $1/2$ inch thick.

5 Place the flattened rolls on a well greased baking sheet, leave to rise again for a further 30 minutes in a warm place, covered with a cloth. Meanwhile, preheat the oven to 400°F.

6 For the topping, cut the grapes in half and press them lightly into each piece of dough. Sprinkle some sugar over. Finally, drizzle the olive oil over, then bake in the oven for 15–20 minutes until the top is slightly crusty. Transfer them to a cooling rack, serve warm or at room temperature.

VARIATIONS

Replace the grapes with dried cherries or cranberries for an interesting variation.

Add fennel seeds to the basic dough to give a savory taste.

For a nutty variation add $2/3$ cup chopped and toasted nuts, such as pine nuts, kneaded into the dough or sprinkled on top, or use untoasted nuts, pressed into the dough before baking.

INGREDIENTS
MAKES 1 LOAF OR
10 SMALL ROUNDS

$4^{1}/_{2}$ cups white bread flour
1 tsp fine sea salt
$1^{1}/_{2}$ tsp active dry ($1/2$ oz fresh) yeast
scant $1/2$ cup sweet white wine
4 tbsp olive oil
scant 1 cup warm water

FOR THE TOPPING
1 lb small red seedless grapes
2 tbsp superfine sugar
4 tbsp olive oil

spiced moroccan kesra

In the Maghreb, folk eat bread with every meal — with a belief that it is a divine gift from God. Harissa is a typical Moroccan spice paste made from chilies, and is available from good delis and leading supermarkets.

1 Sift the flour, cornmeal, and a little salt into a large bowl. In a pitcher mix $1\frac{1}{2}$ cups of the water, the yeast, saffron, harissa, ginger, and sugar. Allow to cool slightly.

2 Make a well in the flour, pour in the saffron and spice liquid along with the melted butter. Using one hand, bring the mix together to form a soft dough. Gradually add the remaining water to form a smooth and pliable dough.

3 Turn the dough out onto a floured surface, knead for 5 minutes, then place back in the bowl, cover with plastic wrap or a damp cloth and leave to rise in a warm place for 1 hour or until doubled in size.

4 Turn out the dough and knock back to expel the air. Gently knead in the fresh cilantro, then shape into 2 neat rounds of equal size.

5 Place on a lightly greased baking sheet, cover again with a cloth and leave to rise again in a warm place for a further 45 minutes or until doubled in size.

6 Preheat the oven to 400°F. Spray the loaves with water and dust with the cracked wheat. Bake on the center shelf for 30 minutes until golden, or hollow sounding when the bottom is tapped. Transfer to a cooling wire to cool.

INGREDIENTS
MAKES 2 LOAVES

5 cups white bread flour
$\frac{3}{4}$ cup fine cornmeal
1 tsp fine sea salt
2 cups warm water
$1\frac{1}{2}$ tsp active dry ($\frac{3}{4}$ oz fresh) yeast
1 tsp powdered saffron or $\frac{1}{2}$ tsp fresh
$\frac{1}{2}$ tsp harissa
3 tsp freshly grated root ginger
1 tbsp superfine sugar
$\frac{1}{4}$ cup unsalted butter, melted, warm
3 tbsp chopped fresh cilantro
2 tbsp cracked wheat

BREAD SALAD, MOROCCAN STYLE

Based on *panzanella*, here is my version — with a Moroccan twist. Serves 4.

Cut 14 oz ripe plum tomatoes in small chunks, place in a colander, sprinkle a little salt over, and leave for 10 minutes; transfer to a large bowl.

Cut one of the *kesra* breads into large chunks, place in a bowl, just cover with cold water and leave for 5 minutes. Squeeze well; add to the tomatoes.

Add 1 large thinly sliced red onion, 4 tbsp chopped fresh cilantro, scant $\frac{1}{2}$ cup olive oil, 1 tsp crushed garlic, 1 chopped red chili, pinch of ground cumin, and $\frac{1}{2}$ tsp chopped root ginger.

Finally add $\frac{1}{4}$ cup red wine vinegar. Mix well and season to taste.

wild herb fougasse

France's answer to Italy's *focaccia*, *fougasse* is a specialty flatbread from Provence. It distinguishes itself from the crowd by its unusual leaf shape and herringbone-style slits down the center. In this recipe I have flavored the bread with the wild herbs typically found in the region.

INGREDIENTS
MAKES 3 LOAVES

6 cups white bread flour
1 tsp fine sea salt
1$\frac{1}{2}$ tsp active dry yeast
2 cups warm water
$\frac{1}{3}$ cup olive oil, plus little extra for brushing
2 tbsp chopped fresh rosemary
1 tbsp chopped fresh mint
2 tbsp picked fresh thyme leaves

1 Sift the flour and salt in a large mixing bowl. Add the yeast. In a pitcher mix the water with the oil. Make a well in the center of the flour. Pour in the oil and water to form a soft dough.

2 Turn out onto a floured surface and knead for 5–6 minutes until smooth and elastic. Place the dough in a lightly oiled bowl, cover with plastic wrap and place in warm place to proof for 1 to 1$\frac{1}{2}$ hours or until doubled in size.

3 Turn out the dough again, work in the herbs and knock back to expel the air. Divide the dough into three pieces. Roll each into an oval about $\frac{3}{4}$ inch thick.

4 Using a sharp knife, cut herring bone-style slashes down the middle of the dough and brush lightly with a little olive oil. Place on 3 baking sheets, lightly dusted with flour, and leave to rise again in a warm place for a further hour. Meanwhile, preheat the oven to 400°F.

5 Bake on the center shelf for 15 minutes until golden. Transfer to cooling wire to cool.

VARIATION

In her fantastic book, *The Bread Book*, Linda Collister suggests a variation of *fougasse* adding candied orange peel and a lighter orange flower water to the dough.

PIZZA TOPPINGS

This basic dough can be topped with all manner of ingredients to form great pizzas, here are my favorites –

Selection of seafood on a tomato passata (canned tomato purée) base, topped with arugula and sour cream

Smoked chicken with red onion and thyme

Sliced cooked potatoes, onions, chopped bacon, and sausage with herbs, topped with Brie cheese.

To my wife and family for continued support with my projects.

Author's acknowledgments

Working on this book has been a real pleasure as always despite the extra pounds I've added to my waistline! I recognise that producing a book like this involves great teamwork, I would like therefore to thank the following people:

Jacqui Small and Kate John for their inspiration and encouragement; Madeline Weston, editor, and Ashley Western, art director, for ultimately making the book look so good; Linda Tubby, home economist and Richard Jung, photographer, for their support and enthusiasm with the project from its initiation, and their friendship; To Roisin Nield, stylist, for sourcing such wonderful props; To Lara King for her continued support and friendship; Chefs Pascal Betesta and Graham Hornigold for help preparing the different breads for photography.

The publisher wishes to thank Divertimenti, 33-34 Marylebone High Street, London, W1H 1AD for the loan of accessories for photography.